I0213931

ABOUT ME

Tinnell Sloan has been creating cookie art for over 6 years. She is the mother of two amazing children, Rilee and Jaxson. She often refers to her cookies as her third child!

What started off as a hobby has grown into a business, Adoughable Cookies, that she is extremely proud of. "Cookies are my love language!"

Her cookie journey has found her baking for various sports teams, celebrities, corporations, birthday parties and baby showers, but her most recent endeavor was as a finalist on Food Network's Christmas Cookie Challenge!

Bird House Publishing
8325 Broadway Street, Pearland, TX 77581
(832) 535-2362

ISBN: 978-1-7343217-2-2

Photography by Kirsten Gilliam
Design Layout: Tamar Tietelbaum

Bird House Publishing rev date 11/28/20

CHRISTMAS COOKIE CUT OUTS

Melting Snowman

"This snowman got a little too close to the fire and is MELTING!"

Ingredients

- Ingredients for your preferred cookies
- Jumbo marshmallows
- Pretzels

First, choose a cookie recipe and follow the directions to make the cookie dough. Next, follow the steps below:

1. Use sharp scissors to cut out 1 shape. This will serve as your cookie cutters. See page 35-46 to learn how to cut shapes into your dough.
2. Bake cookies according to the recipe.
3. Allow time for cookies to cool. Remember to not rush the cool time. If you want to speed up the process, pop the tray in the refrigerator until cookies are cool to the touch.

To assemble:

1. Add icing to your base cookie.
2. While icing is wet, add jumbo marshmallows. (See tips below).
3. Decorate the snowman's face.
4. Add scarf.

Enjoy!

TIPS:

- Prep your jumbo marshmallows by adding pretzels to marshmallow before placing marshmallow on the cookie base.
- Allow 20 minutes of dry time between each step for best results.
- If you want icing to dry faster, place cookies under a fan in between steps.

Santa Puzzle

"This seven-piece Santa puzzle won't confuse you!"

Ingredients

- Ingredients for your preferred cookies
- Candy

First, choose a cookie recipe and follow the directions to make the cookie dough. Next, follow the steps below:

1. Use sharp scissors to cut out 7 shapes. They will serve as your cookie cutters. See page 35-46 to learn how to cut out shapes into your dough.
2. Bake cookies according to the recipe.
3. Allow time for cookies to cool. Remember to not rush cool time. If you want to speed up the process, pop the tray in the refrigerator until cookies are cool to the touch.

To decorate:

1. Outline each shape using icing with a thick consistency. See page 26-28.
2. Flood Santa's face. See page 29-33.
3. Allow 1 hour of dry time before adding his eyes and brows
4. Once all pieces are dry, assemble Santa.

TIPS:

- Use thick consistency icing for Santa's eyes and eyebrows.
- If you want icing to dry faster, place cookies under a fan in between steps.

Giant Gingerbread Man

"Sugar and spice everything nice!"

Ingredients

- Ingredients for your preferred cookies
- Candy

First, choose a cookie recipe and follow the directions to make the cookie dough. Next, follow the steps below:

1. Use sharp scissors to cut out 1 shape. This will serve as your cookie cutter. See page 35-46 to learn how to cut out shapes into your dough.
2. Bake cookies according to the recipe.
3. Allow time for cookies to cool. Remember to not rush cool time. If you want to speed up the process, pop the tray in the refrigerator until cookies are cool to the touch.

To decorate:

1. Outline the cookies.
2. Flood gingerbread man's full body.
3. Allow 20 minutes of dry time.
4. Place a small dot of icing on one side of desired candy to add details

Enjoy!

TIPS:

- Use icing with a for creating details.
- If you want icing to dry faster, place cookies under a fan in between steps.

Nerdy Snowman

"We do not CARROT all about your traditional snowman! This guy is nerdy and nice! "

Ingredients

- Ingredients for your preferred cookies
- Candy

First, choose a cookie recipe and follow the directions to make the cookie dough. Next, follow the steps below:

1. Use sharp scissors to cut out 1 shape. This will serve as your cookie cutter. See page 35-46 to learn how to cut out shapes into your dough.
2. Bake cookies according to the recipe.
3. Allow time for cookies to cool. Remember to not rush cool time. If you want to speed up the process, pop the tray in the refrigerator until cookies are cool to the touch.

To decorate:

Follow the picture guide to see how to decorate!

Enjoy!

TIPS:

- Allow 20 minutes of dry time between each step for best results.
- If you want the icing to dry faster, place cookies under a fan in between steps.

3D Gingerbread Candy House

"Get ready for a good time!
This cute candy house is a candy lover's dream!"

Ingredients

- Ingredients for your preferred cookies
- Candy
- Clear or white sprinkles for snow

First, choose a cookie recipe and follow the directions to make the cookie dough. Next, follow the steps below:

1. Use sharp scissors to cut out 3 shapes. They will serve as your cookie cutters. See page 35-46 to learn how to cut out shapes into your dough.
2. Bake cookies according to the recipe.
3. Allow time for cookies to cool. Remember to not rush cool time. If you want to speed up the process, pop the tray in the refrigerator until cookies are cool to the touch.

To decorate:

1. Place a thick line of icing in the middle of your base.
2. Place house directly on top of the icing line.
3. Add your wedge to help secure the house.
4. Add icing and sprinkles cover to the base.
5. Allow cookies to dry.

Enjoy!

TIPS:

- Use super thick consistency icing as your "glue" when assembling your house to the base.
- If you want icing to dry faster, place cookies under a small fan in between steps.

Picture Frame

"Pictures are worth 1000 words,
but this ADOUGHABLE picture frame is priceless!"

Ingredients

- Ingredients for your preferred cookies
- Candy
- Printed picture

First, choose a cookie recipe and follow the directions to make the cookie dough. Next, follow the steps below:

1. Use sharp scissors to cut out 3 shapes. They will serve as your cookie cutters. See page 35-46 to learn how to cut out shapes into your dough.
2. Bake cookies according to the recipe.
3. Allow time for cookies to cool. Remember to not rush cool time. If you want to speed up the process, pop the tray in the refrigerator until cookies are cool to the touch.

To decorate:

1. Decorate the front of your frame and allow time to dry and set aside.
2. Place a photo on the center of the base.
3. Line the back of the frame with icing.
4. Place the frame on top of the base so that the photo is seen through the window.
5. Add icing to the stand and attach to the back of the base for extra support.

TIPS:

- Use super thick consistency icing as your "glue."
- If you want icing to dry faster, place cookies under a small fan in between steps.

Christmas Wreath

"This cute holiday wreath will look amazing on any dessert table on Christmas day!"

Ingredients

- Ingredients for your preferred cookies
- Candy (Optional)

First, choose a cookie recipe and follow the directions to make the cookie dough. Next, follow the steps below:

1. Use sharp scissors to cut out 6 shapes. They will serve as your cookie cutters. See page 35-46 to learn how to cut out shapes into your dough.
2. Bake cookies according to the recipe.
3. Allow time for cookies to cool. Remember to not rush cool time. If you want to speed up the process, pop the tray in the refrigerator until cookies are cool to the touch.

To decorate:

1. Outline each shape using thick consistency icing.
2. Flood each piece.
3. Allow time for icing to dry.
4. Arrange cookies in a circle.

Enjoy!

TIPS:

- Feel free to embellish your wreath with candy "ornaments" or leave it plain.
- If you decide to add candies to your wreath, place a small drop of icing on one side of the candy before placing it onto your wreath as ornaments.
- If you want icing to dry faster, place cookies under a fan in between steps.

Oh Christmas Tree

"I don't know about you, but decorating the tree is one of my favorite Christmas traditions!"

Ingredients

- Ingredients for your preferred cookies
- Candy

First, choose a cookie recipe and follow the directions to make the cookie dough. Next, follow the steps below:

1. Use sharp scissors to cut out 1 shape. They will serve as your cookie cutters. See page 35-46 to learn how to cut out shapes into your dough.
2. Bake cookies according to the recipe.
3. Allow time for cookies to cool. Remember to not rush cool time. If you want to speed up the process, pop the tray in the refrigerator until cookies are cool to the touch.

To decorate:

Follow the picture guide to see how to decorate!

Enjoy!

TIPS:

- Allow 20 minutes of dry time between each step for best results.
- Use candy or a drop of icing to make your ornaments.
- If you want icing to dry, faster place cookies under a fan in between steps.

Hanging Lights Garland

"Deck the house with hanging cookie lights!"

Ingredients

- Ingredients for your preferred cookies
- String of ribbon

First, choose a cookie recipe and follow the directions to make the cookie dough. Next, follow the steps below:

1. Use sharp scissors to cut out 1 shape. They will serve as your cookie cutters. See page 35-46 to learn how to cut out shapes into your dough.
2. Before baking, use a skewer, toothpick, or piping tip to make a hole in each cookie. (If you forget this step like I do sometimes, put the hole in the cookie immediately after baking and before allowing cookies to cool.
3. Bake cookies according to the recipe.
4. Allow time for cookies to cool. Remember to not rush cool time. If you want to speed up the process, pop the tray in the refrigerator until cookies are cool to the touch.

To decorate:

1. Outline each shape using thick consistency icing.
2. Flood each piece.
3. Allow dry time.
4. Take a string or ribbon and thread through each hole.
5. Hang cookies.

Enjoy!

TIPS:

- Remember to not cover the hole with icing!
- Allow 20 minutes of dry time between each step for best results

Randy the Reindeer

"Meet Randy the Reindeer "

Ingredients

- Ingredients for your preferred cookies
- String of ribbon

First, choose a cookie recipe and follow the directions to make the cookie dough. Next, follow the steps below:

1. Use sharp scissors to cut out 2 shapes. They will serve as your cookie cutters. See page 35-46 to learn how to cut out shapes into your dough.
2. Bake cookies according to the recipe.
3. Allow time for cookies to cool. Remember to not rush cool time. If you want to speed up the process, pop the tray in the refrigerator until cookies are cool to the touch.

1. Outline and flood Randy's face and antlers.
2. Allow 20 minutes of dry time.
3. Add Randy's eyebrows, eyes, and ears.
4. Place a small dot of icing on one side of desired candy to add ornaments to Randy's antlers.
5. Pipe and flood Randy's nose.
6. Add Randy's shiny red nose to his face.

TIPS:

- Bake Randy's nose separately from his face(pay attention to the size difference).
- If you want icing to dry faster, place cookies under a fan in between steps.

ROYAL ICING

Icing! Icing! Icing! I love a good royal icing!

When your cookies are cooling, it is time to get started on the icing. The key to decorating beautiful cookies is your icing. For a beginner, making and decorating with royal icing can be intimidating. Take a deep breath, take a bite of one of your yummy baked cookies, and don't worry because we are in this together! I have provided a recipe for royal icing with meringue powder. This is the only royal icing recipe I use because it is easy to use, does not require raw egg, and won't dry rock hard so it is easy to eat!

RECIPE

Ingredients

- 2lbs of powdered sugar (7 cups)
- 3 tablespoons of meringue powder
- ¾ cup of warm water
- 1 tablespoon of (clear) vanilla extract
- 1 teaspoon of almond extract (optional)
- Gel food coloring

Once you have all your ingredients, follow these easy steps:

1. Mix powdered sugar and meringue powder in the bowl of a stand mixer using whisk attachment on low speed.
2. Pour extracts into the mixing bowl, keeping the mixer on low speed.
3. Scrape side of the bowl, as necessary.
4. When icing is thick and white, separate icing into smaller bowls and add desired gel food colors. Start with a drop or two and stir it in. If you want to intensify the color, add a drop more.
5. Use a spatula to fill colored icing into tipless piping bag then cut a small end of the bag tip.

TIPS:

- Make sure all bowls and utensils are dry and completely free of grease so your icing will reach the desired consistency.
- Consistency is key! Ensure it's the right consistency before adding gel color.

OUTLINING

Think back to when you would color in a coloring book. You traced the picture first (outlining), then you shade it in (flooding). That makes decorating cookies a little easier when you think of it that way! Outlining helps the icing stay on the cookie and keeps it from oozing off the edge. When outlining a cookie with royal icing, place the tip close to the cookie and gently squeeze the piping bag until the icing comes out. Make a small dot as your starting point, lift the tip up and slowly guide the icing in the direction you want it to go.

The tip is lifted about an inch off the cookie, and the icing should be falling along the edge. If your tip is too close to the cookie, you will have an uneven, wiggly line, so make sure you are lifting and gently pulling the icing, letting it fall. By holding the tip up a little, it allows you to outline with control.

OUTLINING

FLOODING

Now that we have the hang of outlining, flooding is the easy part! To flood your cookie, start at the edge of the outline and squeeze the piping bag until the icing comes out. Keep applying pressure to the piping bag as you slowly fill the cookie with icing. You can go from one side to the other or start around the edges and move towards the center. You can't go wrong; just stay in between the outline! Once your cookie is completely flooded, very lightly shake your cookie side to side or tap it on the table to help the icing flatten out. If you have any air bubbles, take a toothpick or skewer on pop them then shake again!

FLOODING

Nerdy Snowman

3D Gingerbread Candy House

Picture Frame

Chrismas Wreath

Oh Christmas Tree

FLOODING

Hanging Lights Garland

Randy the Reindeer

CONSISTENCY

I wish I could be there to help you out because this can be another intimidating part of decorating. But after years and years of decorating, I still have days that my icing consistency isn't perfect. My outline icing is so thick that it sometimes hurts my hand to outline because I'm squeezing so hard! Sometimes I make a common mistake and add too much water, making my flood icing too thin! This is a "practice makes perfect" moment! It's not an exact science!

I generally stick with two consistencies:

- Thick consistency: used for outlining, design details, and to "glue" 3D cookies together. This is a stiff icing.
- Medium consistency: used for flooding. Similar to the consistency of pancake mix, it's not too thick but isn't too runny either.

TIPS:

- To make it thicker add more powdered sugar, to make it thinner add more water!

ALL ABOUT THE DOUGH!

How to "Cut Out"

I love making cut out cookies! They are customizable and allows you to make some unique shapes. In this book Cut Out has a double meaning, we are not only cutting out the shape in the cookie dough, but you'll be cutting out the stencils provided and that will serve as your cookie cutter.

Use a small, sharp knife or I prefer an exacto knife to cut any shape into your rolled-out cookie dough

TIPS:

- After you have cut out your cookies, refrigerate or freeze the unbaked cookies for about 5 to 10 minutes. That extra coolness will help your cookies retain their shape and will keep them from spreading in your hot oven between steps.
- Re-trace the stencil onto cardstock paper. Thicker page will help your "cut out" cookie cutter last longer.

Santa Puzzle

Giant Gingerbread Man

Nerdy Snowman

3D Gingerbread Candy House

Picture Frame

Christmas Wreath

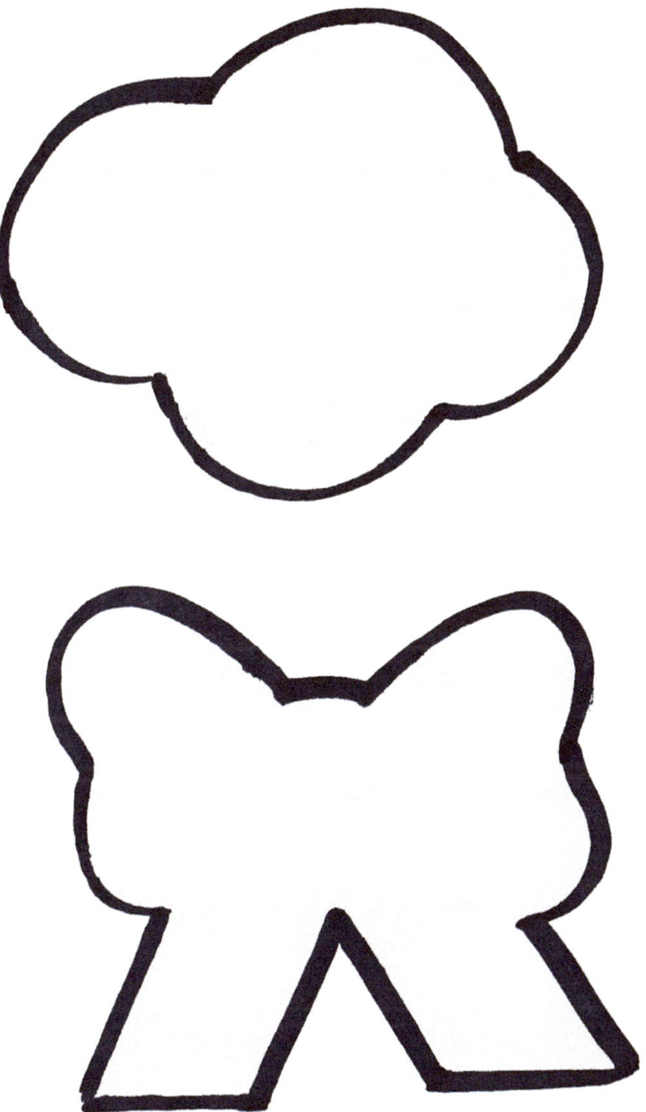

Hanging Lights Garland

Picture Frame

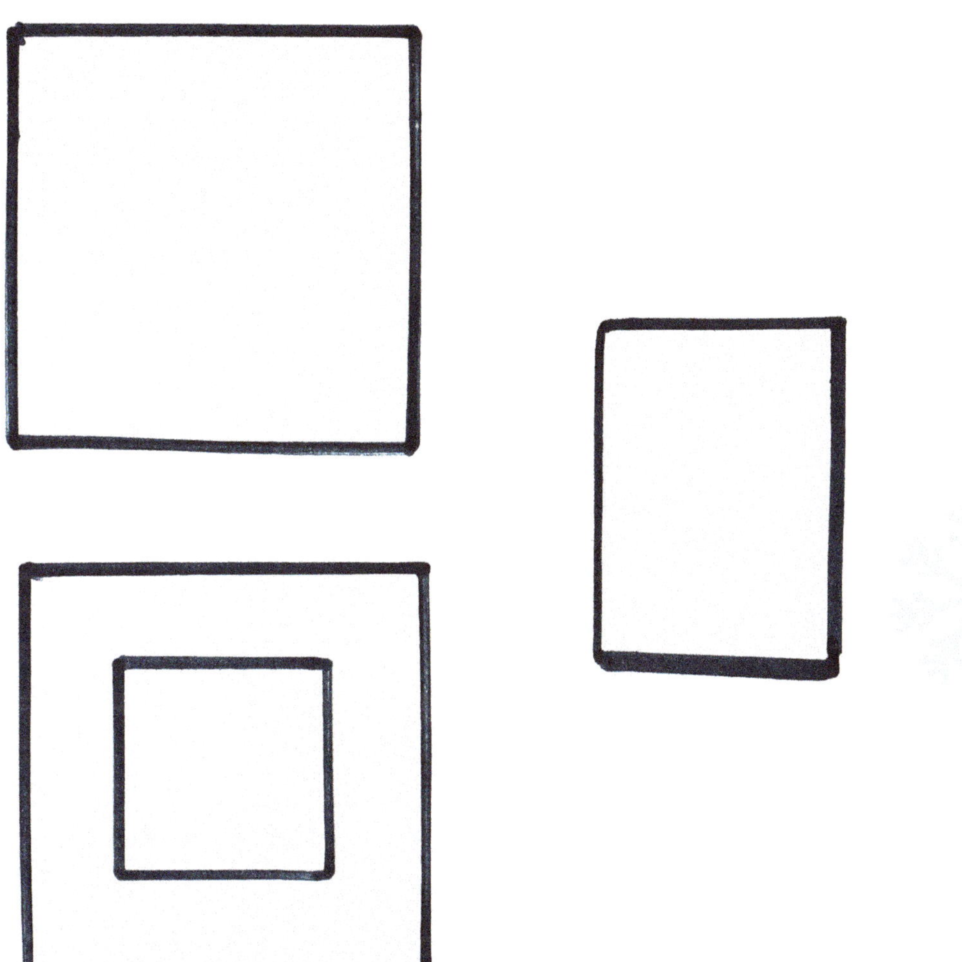

Randy the Reindeer

GOOD LUCK!

COOKIE RECIPES

ADOUGHABLE Cookies Signature Sugar Cookie

INGREDIENTS

- 1 cup of slightly soft salted butter (2 sticks)
- 1 cup of granulated sugar
- 1 large egg
- 1 tbs vanilla extract
- 1 teaspoon almond extract
- 3 - 3 ½ cups of flour

Instructions

1. Preheat the oven to 350°.
2. Prepare baking sheets with parchment paper.
3. Using a stand mixer fitted with the paddle attachment, cream together butter and sugar on medium speed until combined, about 2 minutes.
4. Add egg and extracts and mix until well combined. Scrape the sides of the bowl.
5. Add the flour one cup at a time. You may need to add a little more flour, ½ cup at a time, if the dough is sticky. The dough should form a ball around the paddle and the sides of the bowl should be clean. That is how you know it's ready!
6. On a lightly floured silicon mat or clean countertop, roll out dough to ¼ inch thickness.
7. Use your cut-out stencil and cut shape into the dough. Re-roll the remaining dough and continue cutting until you have all the shapes you need.
8. Arrange cookies on the baking sheet about ½ in to 1 in apart.
9. Bake one sheet at a time in the middle rack of the oven for 11 minutes. The tops of the cookie should appear dry, not shiny, and be nice and puffy.
10. Allow the cookies to cool before decorating.

TIPS:

- Dust spatula with flour to prevent sticking.
- Place a piece of wax paper in between dough and rolling pin for a smoother top.
- After you have cut out the cookies, refrigerate unbaked cookies for 5 to 10 minutes. The extra coolness will help your cookies keep their shape and keep them from spreading.
- If you want crunchier cookies bake until edges are golden brown.
- Pop cookies into the refrigerator for 5 minutes after baking to help them cool off faster.

Cinnamon Brown Sugar Cookie

INGREDIENTS

- 1 cup of slightly soft salted butter (2 sticks)
- 1/2 cup of granulated sugar
- 1 cup of brown sugar
- 1 teaspoon of cinnamon
- 1 large egg
- 2 tbs vanilla extract
- 3 - 3 ½ cups of flour

Instructions

1. Pre-heat the oven to 350°.
2. Prepare baking sheets with parchment paper.
3. Using a stand mixer fitted with the paddle attachment, cream together butter, sugars, and cinnamon on medium speed until combined, about 2 minutes.
4. Add egg and extract and mix until well combined. Scrape the sides of the bowl.
5. Add the flour one cup at a time. You may need to add a little more flour, ½ cup at a time, if the dough is sticky. The dough should form a ball around the paddle and the sides of the bowl should be clean. That is how you know it's ready!
6. On a lightly floured silicon mat or clean countertop, roll out dough to ¼ inch thickness.
7. Use your cut-out stencil and cut shape into the dough. Re-roll the remaining dough and continue cutting until you have all the shapes you need.
8. Arrange cookies on the baking sheet about ½ in to 1 in apart.
9. Bake one sheet at a time in the middle rack of the oven for 11 minutes. The tops of the cookie should appear dry, not shiny, and be nice and puffy.
10. Allow the cookies to cool down before decorating.

TIPS:

- Dust spatula with flour to prevent sticking.
- Place a piece of wax paper in between dough and rolling pin for a smoother top.
- After you have cut out the cookies, refrigerate unbaked cookies for 5 to 10 minutes. The extra coolness will help your cookies keep their shape and keep them from spreading.
- If you want crunchier cookies, bake until edges are golden brown.
- Pop cookies into the refrigerator for 5 minutes after baking to help them cool off faster.

Cinnamon Brown Sugar Oatmeal Cookie

INGREDIENTS

- 1 cup salted butter
- 1 ¼ cup of brown sugar
- 1 cup of sugar
- 1 tsp of cinnamon
- 2 large eggs
- 2 tbs vanilla extract
- 2 ¼ cups of all purpose flour
- 2 tsp baking soda
- ½ tsp of baking powder
- 2 cups of old fashioned oats
- Optional: 1 cup of raisin

Instructions

1. Pre-heat the oven to 350°.
2. Prepare baking sheets with parchment paper
3. Using a stand mixer, fitted with the paddle attachment, cream the butter, sugars and cinnamon on medium speed until combined.
4. Add eggs and vanilla and mixed until well combined.
5. Add flour, baking soda and powder. Then mix. Add oats. The dough should form a ball around the paddle and the sides of the bowl should be clean. Thats how you know its ready.
6. Scoop out dough and roll into a tablespoon size balls. The bigger the ball the bigger the cookie!
7. Arrange cookies onto baking sheet about 2 inches apart.
8. Bake for 7 to 10 minutes until edges are golden brown.
9. Allow cookies to cool.

TIPS:

- This cookie recipe is not recommended to use for cut out shapes. That is why we are rolling them into balls and allowing them to spread while baking.
- Oatmeal cookie center may appear a little underdone in the center, its ok! They are fine.
- For a crispier cookie, bake a little longer.

Smore Holiday Fun Cookie

INGREDIENTS

- 1 cup of slightly soft salted butter (2 sticks)
- 1 cup of granulated sugar
- ½ cup of brown sugar
- 1 large egg
- 2 tbs vanilla extract
- ½ cup chopped graham crackers
- 1 cup semi-sweet chocolate chip
- 1 cup mini marshmallows
- 2 cups of flour

Instructions

1. Pre-heat the oven to 350°.
2. Prepare baking sheets with parchment paper.
3. Using a stand mixer fitted with the paddle attachment, cream together butter and sugars on medium speed until combined, about 2 minutes.
4. Add egg and extract and mix until well combined. Scrape the sides of the bowl.
5. Add chopped graham crackers, chocolate chips and marshmallows.
6. Add the flour one cup at a time. You may need to add a little more flour, ½ cup at a time, if the dough is sticky. The dough should form a ball around the paddle and the sides of the bowl should be clean. That is how you know it's ready!
7. On a lightly floured silicon mat or clean countertop, roll into tablespoon size balls. The bigger the ball the bigger the cookie!
8. Use your cut-out stencil and cut shape into the dough. Re-roll the remaining dough and continue cutting until you have all the shapes you need.
9. Arrange cookies on the baking sheet about ½ in to 1 in apart.
10. Bake one sheet at a time in the middle rack of the oven for 11 minutes. The tops of the cookie should appear dry, not shiny, and be nice and puffy.
11. Allow the cookies to cool down before decorating.

TIPS:

- This cookie recipe is not recommended to use for cut-out shapes because of the chocolate chips. That is why we are rolling them into a ball and allowing them to spread while baking.
- Before baking you can top your cookies with more marshmallows and chocolate!
- If you want crunchier cookies, bake until edges are golden brown.
- Pop cookies into the refrigerator for 5 minutes after baking to help them cool off faster.

Chocolate Peppermint Cookie

INGREDIENTS

- 1 cup of slightly soft salted butter (2 sticks)
- 1 cup of granulated sugar
- ½ cup of brown sugar
- 1 large egg
- ¼ tsp peppermint extract
- ⅓ cup cocoa powder
- 3 cups of all-purpose flour

Instructions

1. Preheat the oven to 350°.
2. Prepare baking sheets with parchment paper.
3. Using a stand mixer fitted with the paddle attachment, cream together butter and sugars on medium speed until combined, about 2 minutes.
4. Add egg and extract and mix until well combined. Scrape the sides of the bowl.
5. Add cocoa powder.
6. Add the flour one cup at a time. You may need to add a little more flour, ½ cup at a time, if the dough is sticky. The dough should form a ball around the paddle and the sides of the bowl should be clean. That is how you know it's ready!
7. On a lightly floured silicon mat or clean countertop, roll out dough to ¼ inch thickness.
8. Use your cut-out stencil and cut shape into the dough. Re-roll the remaining dough and continue cutting until you have all the shapes you need.
9. Arrange cookies on the baking sheet about ½ in to 1 in apart.
10. Bake one sheet at a time in the middle rack of the oven for 11 minutes. The tops of the cookie should appear dry, not shiny, and be nice and puffy.
11. Allow the cookies to cool down before decorating.

TIPS:

- Dust spatula with flour to prevent sticking.
- Place a piece of wax paper in between dough and rolling pin for a smoother top
- After you have cut out, refrigerate unbaked cookies for 5 to 10 minutes. The extra coolness will help your cookies keep their shape and keep them from spreading in the oven
- Pop cookies into the refrigerator for 5 minutes after baking to help them cool off faster
- Add chopped chunks of peppermint candy for more peppermint taste!

Gingerbread Spice Cookie

INGREDIENTS

- 1 cup of slightly soft salted butter (2 sticks)
- 1 cup of granulated sugar
- ½ cup brown sugar
- 1 large egg
- ½ cup unsulfured molasses
- 2 tbs vanilla
- 1 tbs ground ginger
- ¾ tsp ground cloves
- ½ teaspoon nutmeg
- 1 tbs cinnamon
- 3 - 3 ½ cups of flour
- zest of one small orange (optional)

Instructions

1. Preheat the oven to 350°.
2. Prepare baking sheets with parchment paper.
3. Using a stand mixer fitted with the paddle attachment, cream together butter and sugars on medium speed until combined, about 2 minutes.
4. Add egg, molasses, and extract and mix until well combined. Scrape the sides of the bowl.
5. Add ground ginger, ground cloves, nutmeg, and cinnamon.
6. Add the flour one cup at a time. You may need to add a little more flour, ½ cup at a time, if the dough is sticky. The dough should form a ball around the paddle and the sides of the bowl should be clean. That is how you know it's ready!
7. On a lightly floured silicon mat or clean countertop, roll out dough to ⅛ inch thickness.
8. Use your cut-out stencil and cut shape into the dough. Re-roll the remaining dough and continue cutting until you have all the shapes you need.
9. Arrange cookies on the baking sheet about ½ in to 1 in apart
10. Bake one sheet at a time in the middle rack of the oven for 11 minutes. The tops of the cookie should appear dry, not shiny, and be nice and puffy.
11. Allow the cookies to cool down before decorating.

TIPS:

- Dust spatula with flour to prevent sticking.
- Place a piece of wax paper in between dough and rolling pin for a smoother top.
- After you have cut out the cookies, refrigerate unbaked cookies for 5 to 10 minutes. The extra coolness will help your cookies keep their shape and keep them from spreading.
- Pop cookies into the refrigerator for 5 minutes after baking to help them cool off faster

Chocolate Sugar Cookie

INGREDIENTS

- 1 cup of slightly soft salted butter (2 sticks)
- 1 ½ cups of granulated sugar
- 1 large egg
- 2 tbs vanilla
- ⅔ cup of cocoa powder
- 3 cups of all-purpose flour

Instructions

1. Preheat the oven to 350°.
2. Prepare baking sheets with parchment paper.
3. Using a stand mixer fitted with the paddle attachment, cream together butter and sugar on medium speed until combined, about 2 minutes.
4. Add egg and extract and mix until well combined. Scrape the sides of the bowl.
5. Add cocoa powder.
6. Add the flour one cup at a time. You may need to add a little more flour, ½ cup at a time, if the dough is sticky. The dough should form a ball around the paddle and the sides of the bowl should be clean. That is how you know it's ready!
7. On a lightly floured silicon mat or clean countertop, roll out dough to ¼ inch thickness.
8. Use your cut-out stencil and cut shape into the dough. Re-roll the remaining dough and continue cutting until you have all the shapes you need.
9. Arrange cookies on the baking sheet about ½ in to 1 in apart.
10. Bake one sheet at a time in the middle rack of the oven for 11 minutes. The tops of the cookie should appear dry, not shiny, and be nice and puffy.
11. Allow the cookies to cool down before decorating.

TIPS:

- Dust spatula with flour to prevent sticking.
- Place a piece of wax paper in between dough and rolling pin for a smoother top.
- After you have cut out the cookies, refrigerate unbaked cookies for 5 to 10 minutes. The extra coolness will help your cookies keep their shape and keep them from spreading.
- Pop cookies into the refrigerator for 5 minutes after baking to help them cool off faster

Key Lime White Chocolate Chip Cookie

INGREDIENTS

- 1 cup of slightly soft salted butter (2 sticks)
- 1 cup of granulated sugar
- ½ cup brown sugar
- 1 large egg
- 1 tbsp vanilla
- 2 drops of green food color
- 1 teaspoon spoon key lime zest
- 3 tablespoon lime juice
- 2 cups of white chocolate chips
- 3 - 3 ½ cups of all-purpose flour

Instructions

1. Preheat the oven to 350°.
2. Prepare baking sheets with parchment paper.
3. Using a stand mixer fitted with the paddle attachment, cream together butter and sugars on medium speed until combined, about 2 minutes.
4. Add egg and extract and mix until well combined. Scrape the sides of the bowl.
5. Add two drops of green food color, lime zest, and lime juice. Mix well.
6. Add white chocolate chips and mix well.
7. Add the flour one cup at a time. You may need to add a little more flour, ½ cup at a time, if the dough is sticky. The dough should form a ball around the paddle and the sides of the bowl should be clean. That is how you know it's ready!
8. On a lightly floured silicon mat or clean countertop, roll into tablespoon size balls. The bigger the ball the bigger the cookie!
9. Arrange cookies on the baking sheet about 2 inches apart.
10. Bake one sheet at a time in the middle rack of the oven for 10 minutes. The tops of the cookie should appear dry, not shiny, and be nice and puffy.
11. Allow the cookies to cool down before decorating.

TIPS:

- This cookie recipe is not recommended to use for cut-out shapes because of the white chocolate chips. That is why we are rolling them into a ball and allowing them to spread while baking.
- Before baking, you can top with white chocolate chips!
- If you want crunchier cookies, bake until edges are golden brown.
- Sprinkle lemon zest on top.

Cinnamon Double Chocolate Pecan Chunky Cookie

INGREDIENTS

- 1 cup of slightly soft salted butter (2 sticks)
- 1 cup of granulated sugar
- ½ cup of light brown sugar
- 1 tsp cinnamon
- 1 large egg
- 2 tbs vanilla extract
- ½ cup chopped pecans
- 1 cup semi-sweet chocolate chips
- 1 cup white chocolate chips
- 2 ½ cups of all-purpose flour

Instructions

1. Preheat the oven to 350°.
2. Prepare baking sheets with parchment paper.
3. Using a stand mixer fitted with the paddle attachment, cream together butter, sugars, and cinnamon on medium speed until combined, about 2 minutes.
4. Add egg and extract and mix until well combined. Scrape the sides of the bowl.
5. Add pecans, chocolate chips, and white chocolate chips.
6. Add the flour one cup at a time. You may need to add a little more flour, ½ cup at a time, if the dough is sticky. The dough should form a ball around the paddle and the sides of the bowl should be clean. That is how you know it's ready!
7. On a lightly floured silicon mat or clean countertop, roll into tablespoon size balls. The bigger the ball the bigger the cookie!
8. Arrange cookies on the baking sheet about 2 inches apart.
9. Bake one sheet at a time in the middle rack of the oven for 10 minutes. The tops of the cookie should appear dry, not shiny, and be nice and puffy.
10. Allow the cookies to cool down before decorating.

TIPS:

- This cookie recipe is not recommended to use for cut-out shapes because of the chocolate chips and pecans. That is why we are rolling them into a ball and allowing them to spread while baking!
- Before baking, you can top your cookies with chocolate!
- If you want crunchier cookies, bake until edges are golden brown.
- Pop cookies into the refrigerator for 5 minutes after baking to help them cool off faster.

Enjoy, but most
importantly have fun!!!

ACKNOWLEDGEMENTS

Dedicated to my awesome kiddos, Rilee and Jaxson. I pray that I inspire you to always be creative and to know that you can do anything you put your mind to. Mommy loves you!

Thank you to all my friends, family and neighbors who supported me by being guinea pigs for my recipes. Thanks for staying up late nights, listening to my ideas, and letting me talk about my cookies all day and night! I could not have written my first book without you all.

Thank you! Let's do our happy dance and eat cookies!

www.ingramcontent.com/pod-product-compliance
Lightning Source LLC
Chambersburg PA
CBHW040314100426
42811CB00012B/1445

* 9 7 8 1 7 3 4 3 2 1 7 2 2 *